About The Author

Kaylyn Garcia, 24, of Calvert County, Maryland, was born to share her unique creativity. As a child, she created projects that expressed her passion. These projects continued as she grew, and this book is the culmination of her passion for helping others and the love she has for her soul sister, Leah Foster.
"Fristers" is the first of many books that will feature Leah. Her greatest hope is that these books can help others by demonstrating that brighter days will shine through when we lose someone very special: it just takes a little creativity!
She loves being with her friends and family in her spare time, especially her niece, Leah's beautiful daughter, London Kole.

-Isabella Pessagno, Carly White, Lina Arroyo.

Dedication

To London Kole, you are loved. You are beautiful. You are strong. Never let anyone steal your sparkle. I love you.

Acknowledgment

I would like to take this time to thank not only God, my family, and friends, but my community. I have received so much love and support from all of you in helping keep Leah's memory alive.

Below is a short but sweet list of a few people that have helped me achieve this goal in a number of different ways, for you all I will forever be grateful.

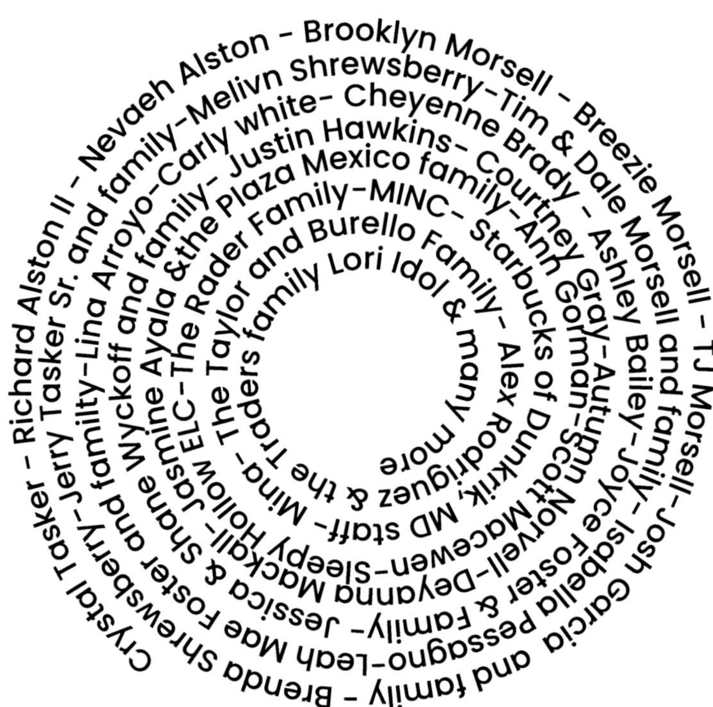

ISBN : 978-1-915165-12-1

Mermaid Publishers
www.mermaidpublishers.com

School

Arriving at school for their
fourth grade year,
there were 2 little girls
filled with cheer.
One silly blonde and one
whacky brunette
were about to form a bond
they wouldn't forget.

School

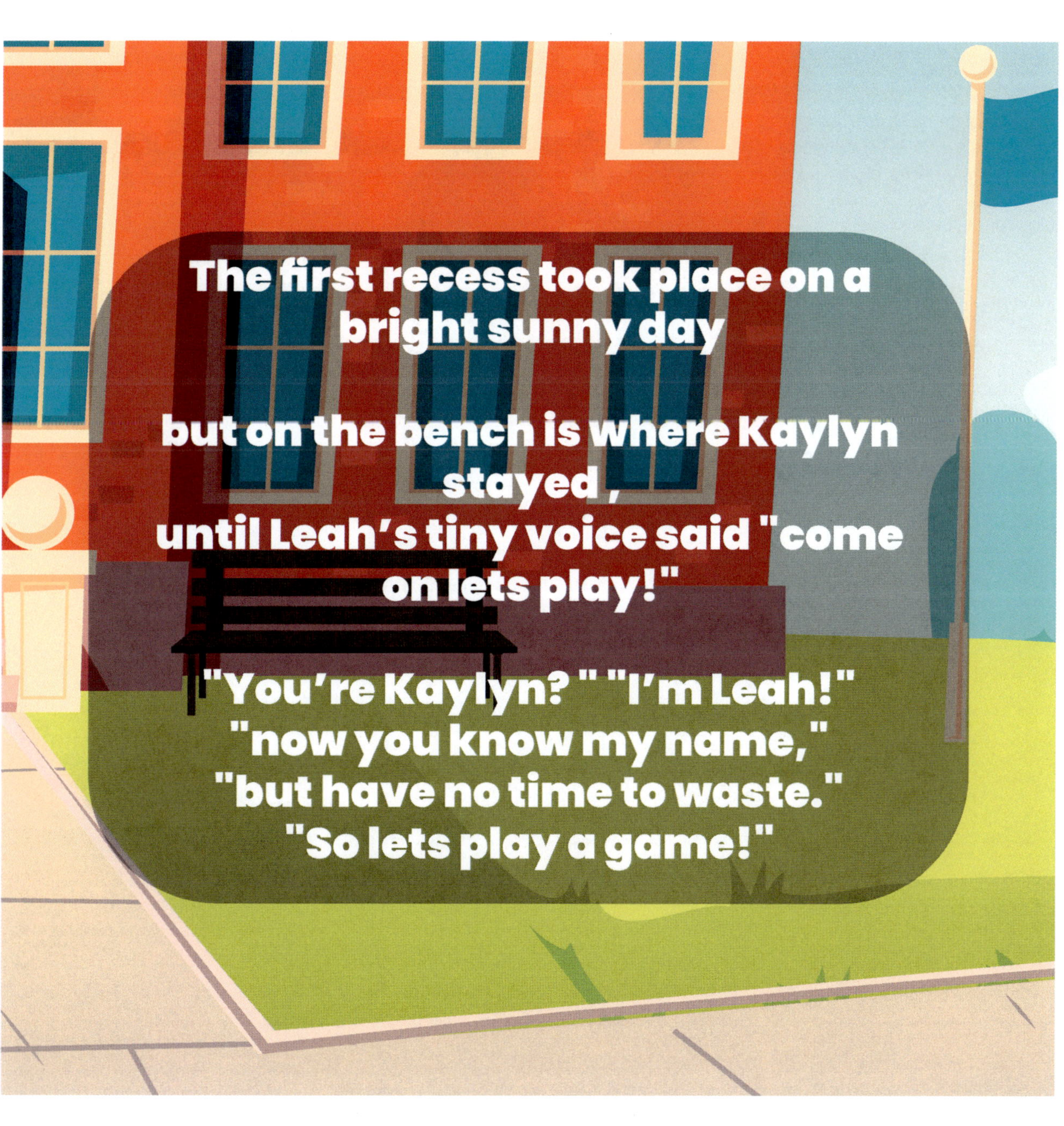
The first recess took place on a bright sunny day
but on the bench is where Kaylyn stayed ,
until Leah's tiny voice said "come on lets play!"
"You're Kaylyn? " "I'm Leah!"
"now you know my name,"
"but have no time to waste."
"So lets play a game!"

8:15

Leah said "sit by me in Mrs. Idol's class"
And a note she did pass,
with the digits to her phone number.

"Lets do a play date tonight."
"It will only be right!"
"If you don't come, it will sure be a bummer!"

And thats when it started,when it all began,
the two best friends that turned into fam,
so close - you'd think they were sisters.

A bond you couldn't break,
a friendship you couldn't replace,

sisters? friends? We'll call them fristers!

Beach Babies Public Schools

Inseparable from one another ,
always there for each other
they chose to be family.
Making forts with the covers,
bus rides to
Leah's grandmother's,
soul sisters they came to be.

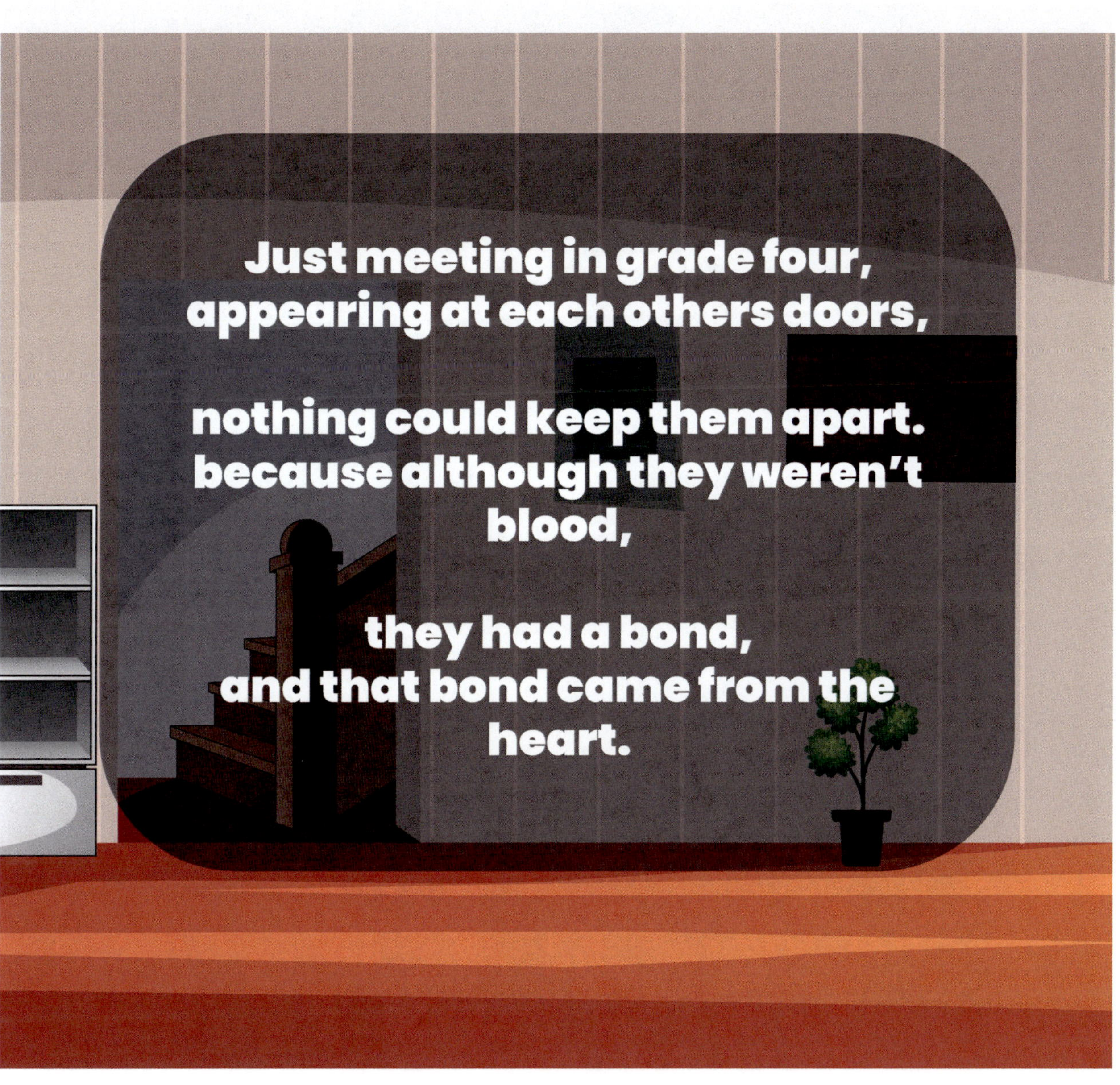
Just meeting in grade four,
appearing at each others doors,

nothing could keep them apart.
because although they weren't
blood,

they had a bond,
and that bond came from the
heart.

They skated, they cooked,and they went to fairs.

They baked, they painted, and styled each other's hair.

They played computer games, danced, and stayed up all night.

Oh, these two together were really a sight!

SCHOOL

Leah and Kaylyn grew older and
to middle school they went ,
the dynamic duo them
two. You never saw one
without the other,
they stayed with each other,
the older they got the closer
they grew.

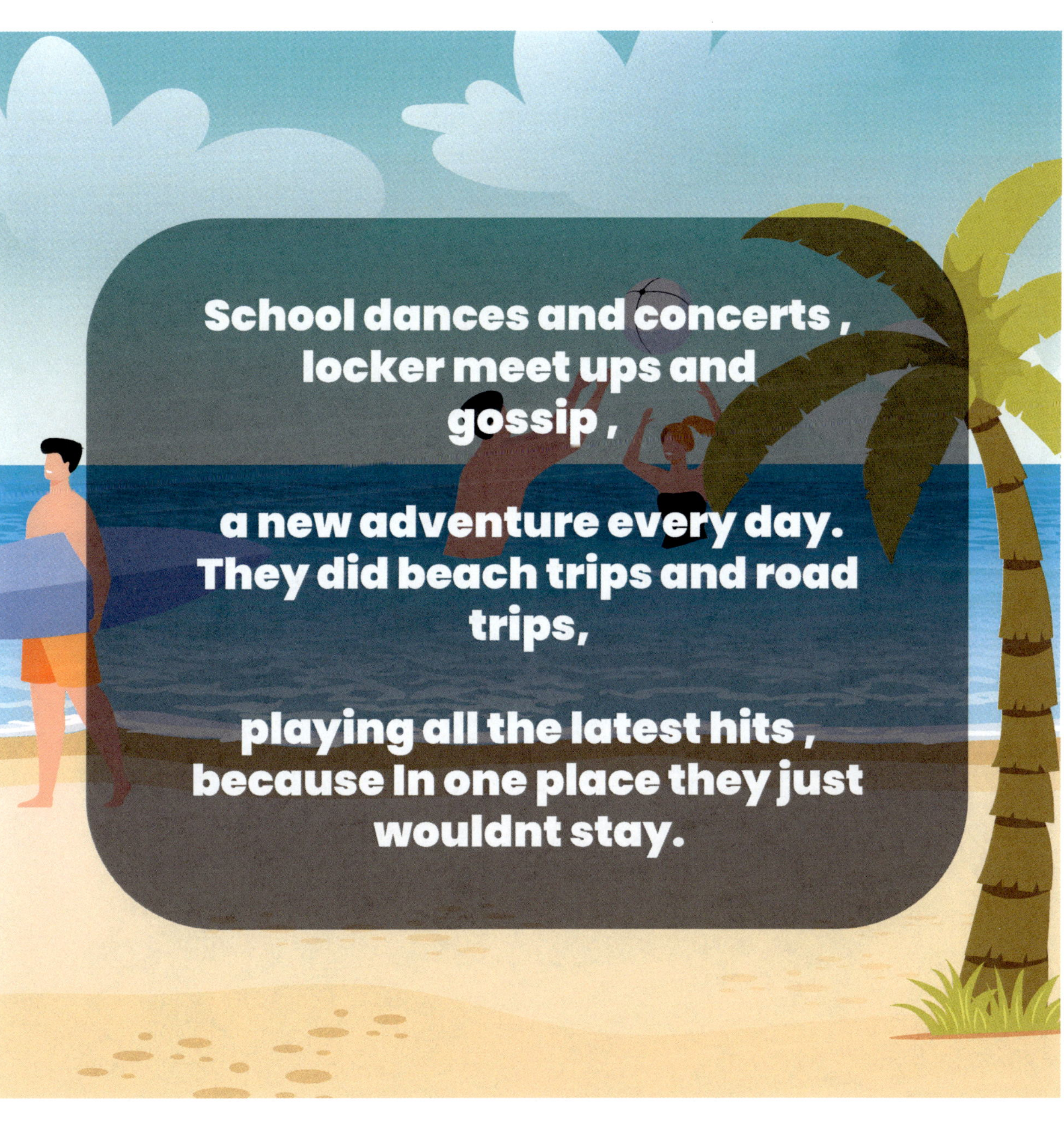
School dances and concerts ,
locker meet ups and
gossip ,

a new adventure every day.
They did beach trips and road
trips,

playing all the latest hits ,
because In one place they just
wouldnt stay.

Highschool became their new home,
teenagers chatting on the phone,
Just keeping up with the latest news.
But their friendship remained the same,
they went to every football game,
while riding home listening to the newest tunes.

Well one day you see,
there was news for them two.

Do you know what it could be?
Now listen to me,

I'll give you a clue
on how the friendship of
just two became a
friendship of three!

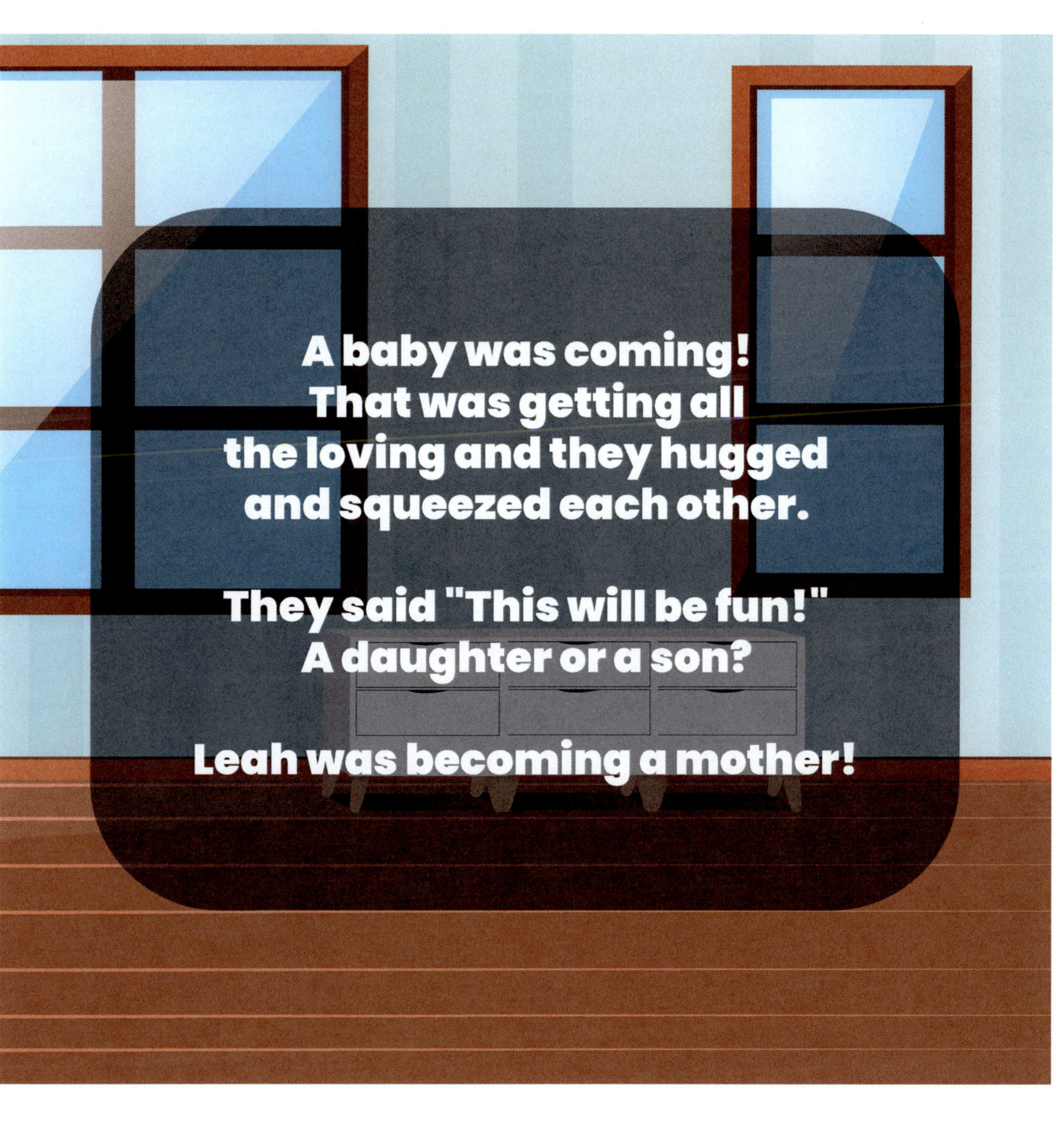
A baby was coming!
That was getting all
the loving and they hugged
and squeezed each other.
They said "This will be fun!"
A daughter or a son?
Leah was becoming a mother!

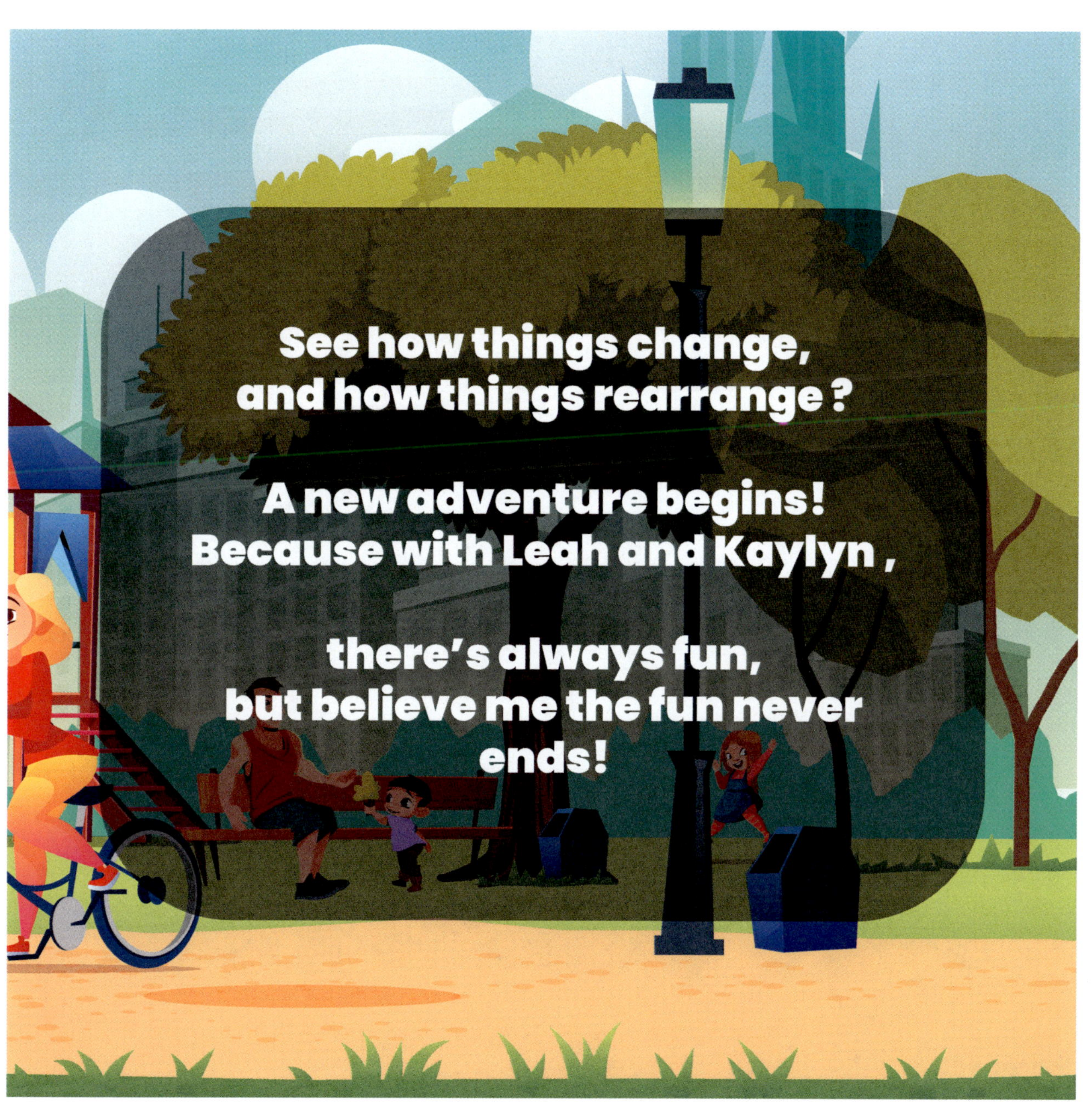
See how things change,
and how things rearrange ?
A new adventure begins!
Because with Leah and Kaylyn ,
there's always fun,
but believe me the fun never
ends!

A quick hospital trip
like a flip of a switch
a little girl joined
their team.

She had the cutest little nose,
the tiniest toes , and the best
eyebrows you'd ever seen.

A pretty little lady,
one beautiful baby
London was truly a dream!

London grew tall ,
and from the time she
was small ,

she had tagged along for
every surprise .

She had seen it all,
they did trips to the mall,

the sweetest girl with the
biggest brown eyes!

SALE
50%

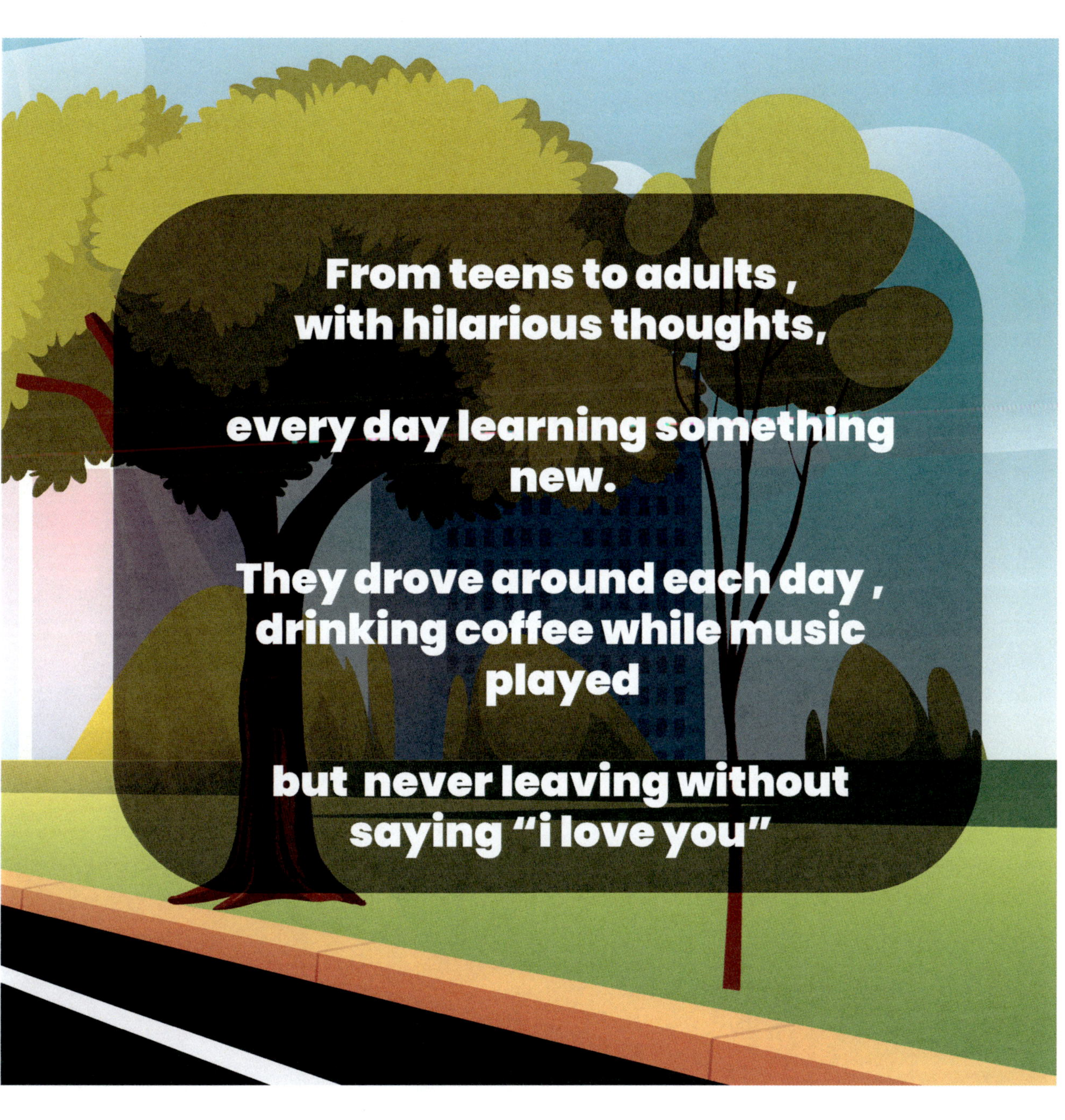
From teens to adults ,
with hilarious thoughts,
every day learning something
new.
They drove around each day ,
drinking coffee while music
played
but never leaving without
saying "i love you"

ZOOLAND
SALE
-20%
STARBUCKS
COFFEE

Sisters by choice rather than blood with a bond formed out of pure love doing most of their hanging out in the car.
Maturing and adulting more each day, looking at each other they would say
"wow have we really came this far?"

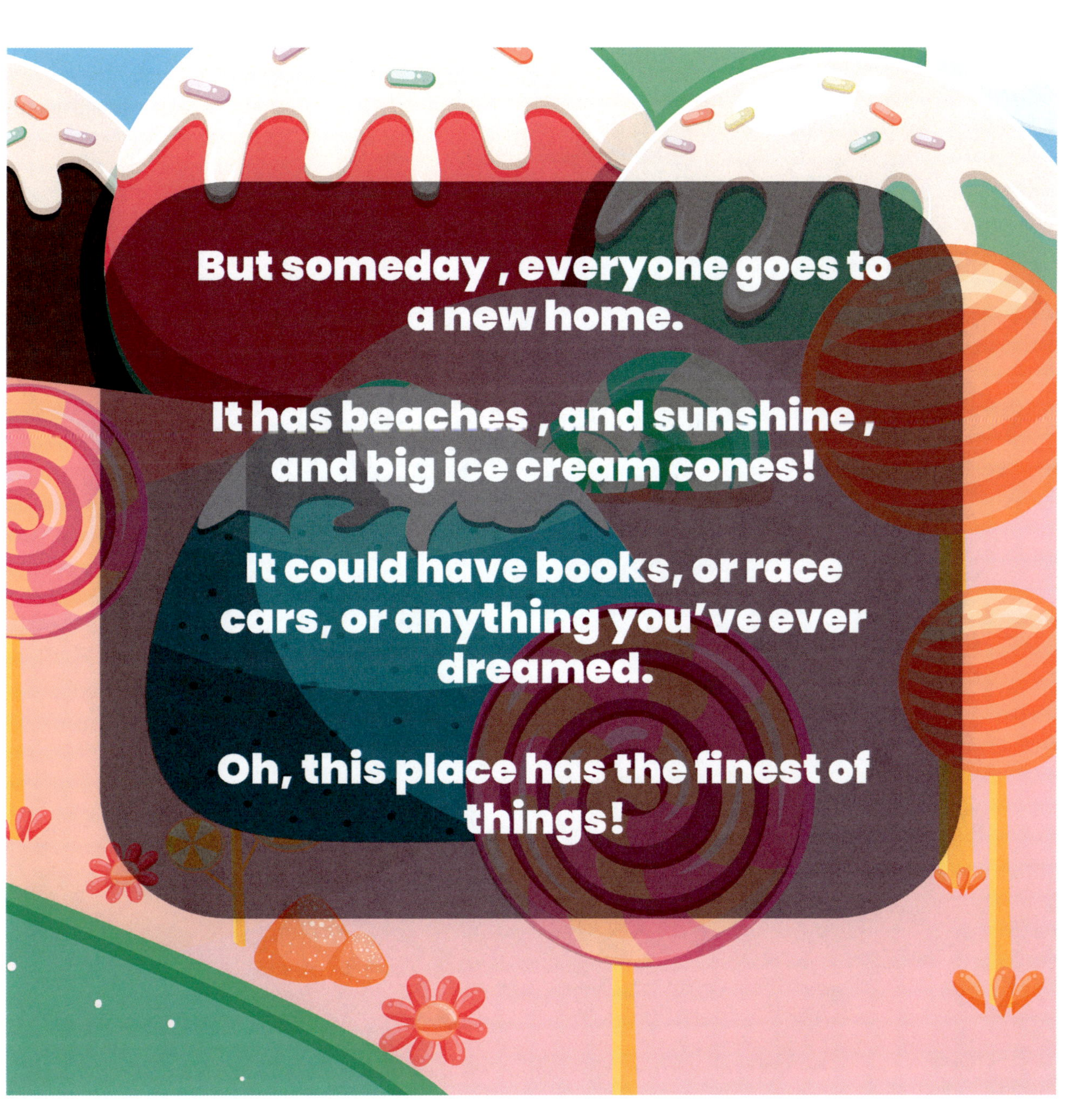

But someday , everyone goes to a new home.

It has beaches , and sunshine , , and big ice cream cones!

It could have books, or race cars, or anything you've ever dreamed.

Oh, this place has the finest of things!

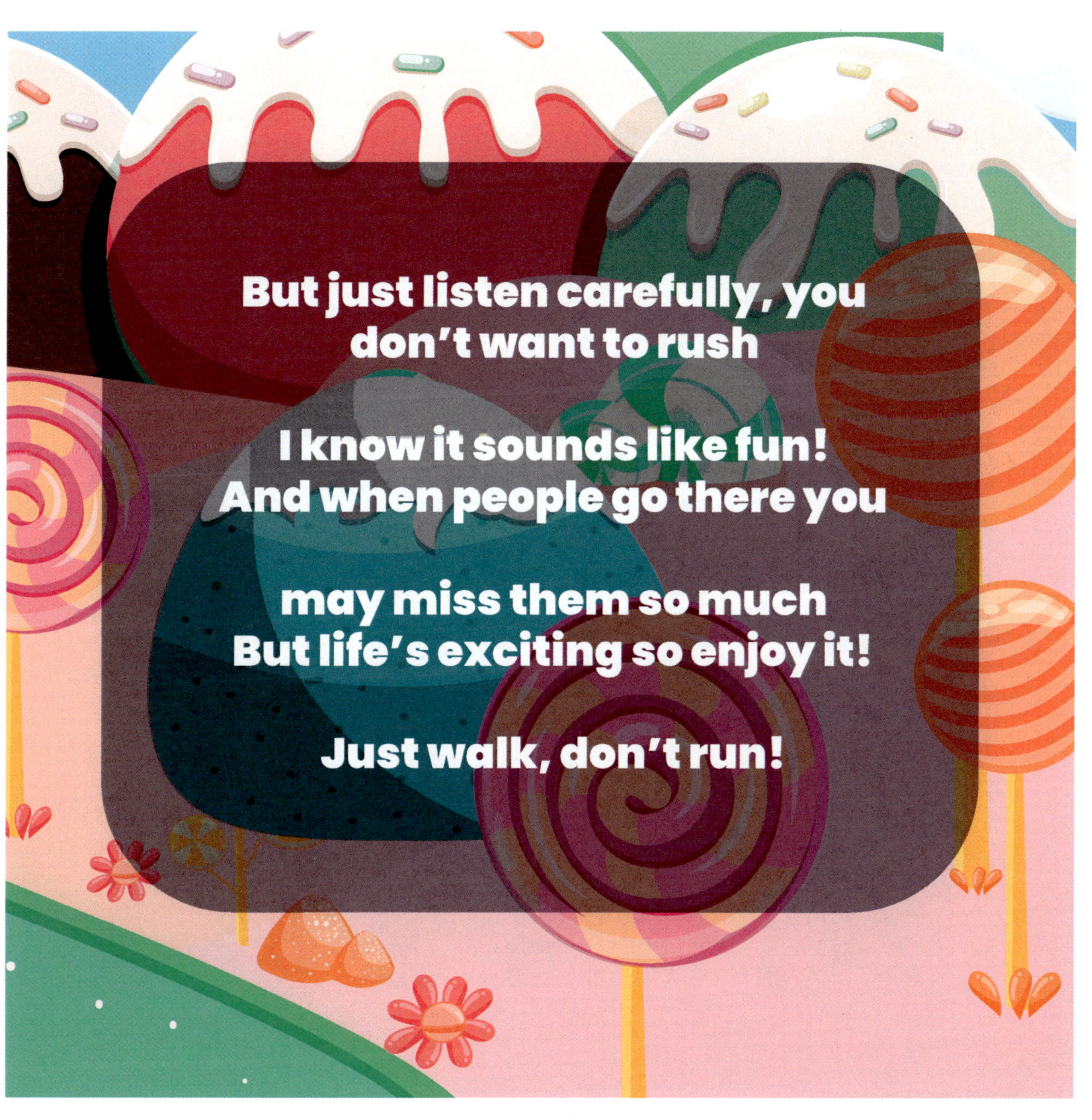
But just listen carefully, you
don't want to rush

I know it sounds like fun!
And when people go there you

may miss them so much
But life's exciting so enjoy it!

Just walk, don't run!

When someone is called home, they might have big events.
People will come together and speak of how their times together were spent.
People will laugh, cry , smile, kiss or hug.
These gatherings show you how much they were loved!

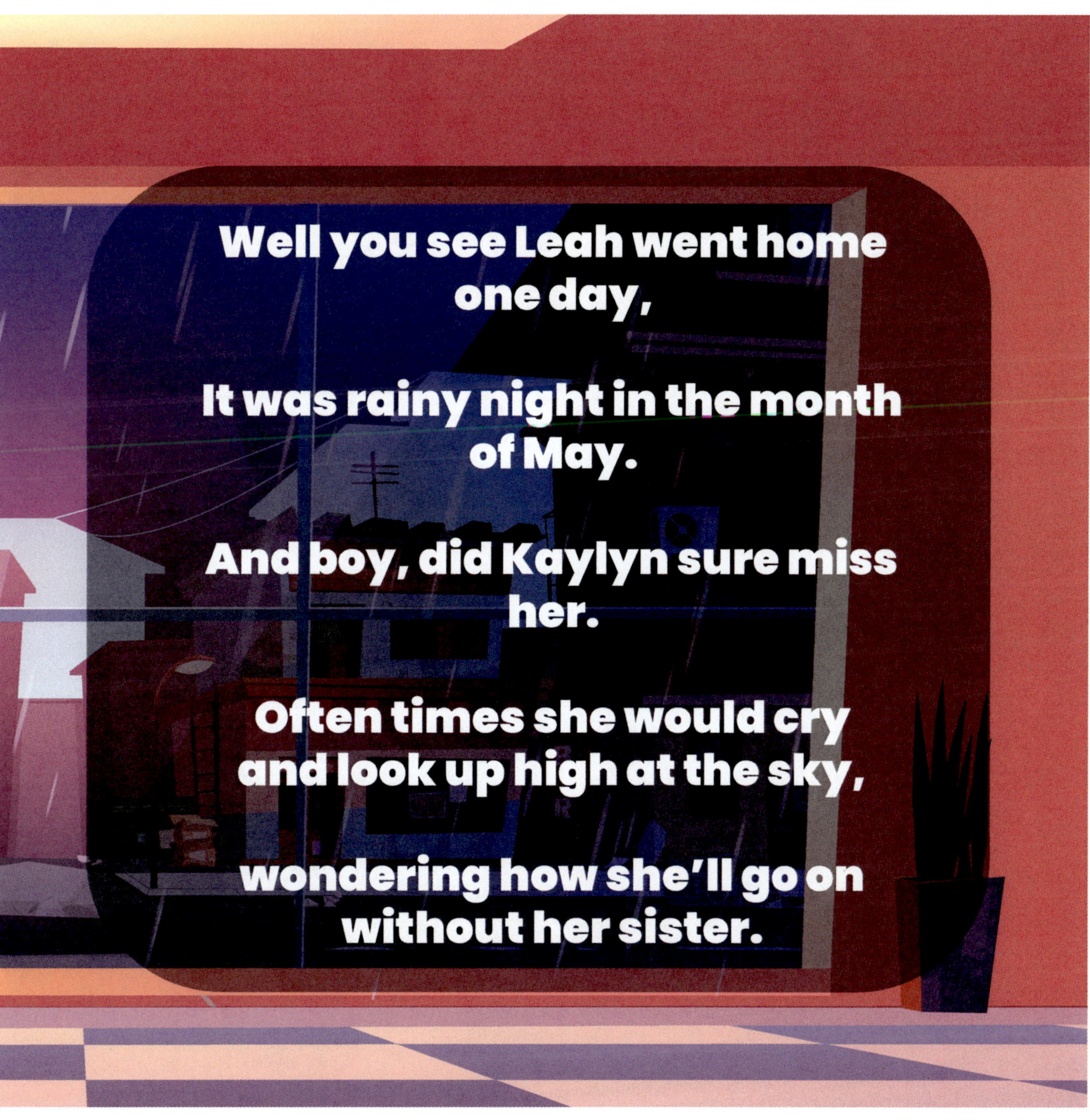

Well you see Leah went home one day,

It was rainy night in the month of May.

And boy, did Kaylyn sure miss her.

Often times she would cry and look up high at the sky,

wondering how she'll go on without her sister.

Those events you ask , oh did
leah have one?
Of course she did , and it was a
ton of fun!
They dressed in purple and
white and decorated with
sunflowers.
It was a gorgeous sight, they
sang and danced for hours!
There were videos, pictures,
and beautiful words were
spoken,
because celebrating life is
beautiful, although your heart
feels broken.

So if you lose someone, you don't have to worry.
I know you don't want to be apart.
But you're here right now , so tell their story
because they'll always be here, just now they're in your heart.

Made in the USA
Coppell, TX
19 May 2022